GW00838682

Dreams of May

A Play with Poetry

by

Sue Guiney

To Leah,

And a future of sharing
work and friendship.

All the best,

Sue

Published by the bluechrome 2006

2 4 6 8 10 9 7 5 3 1

First published in Great Britain in 2006 by
bluechrome publishing
PO Box 109,
Portishead, Bristol. BS20 7ZJ

www.bluechrome.co.uk

A CIP catalogue record for this book is available from the
British Library

ISBN   1-904781-98-5

Dreams of May

A Play with Poetry

Acknowledgements

Acknowledgements are due to the editors of the following publications where some of these poems first appeared, sometimes in slightly different form:
The North American Review, Acumen, The South, Dream Catcher, Vineyard Poets, Martha's Vineyard Magazine, Green's.

The author would also like to express her heartfelt thanks to the Chilmark Poets Writing Group for their support and good-humoured doctoring; to Catherine Harvey, Kay Matschullat, and Caroline Van Valkenburgh for their insightful readings of early drafts; and to Stan Ratoff and Sonja Rein for turning the vision into reality.

Dedication

To my family and friends who refused not to believe
and, most especially, to Verity Langley

Introduction

Over the years, I discovered a funny thing about my poems. The ones which are the most powerful on the page, experienced by a solitary reader alone in a bedroom or on the beach, are not necessarily the ones that move people to stand and applaud at a poetry reading. The ones that a listener remembers long after the reading is over will not necessarily ever get published. And isn't that one of the wonders of poetry? What other medium can grab you in so many different ways via so many different senses? You can see a poem, hear a poem, speak a poem, feel it in a book with your fingers, remember it in your heart through your memory. Clearly, I am not the first to make this discovery. But it is a discovery which drew me to an art form that seems to be, if not forgotten, then often overlooked – the "poetry play."

Dreams of May is just such a play, placing a cycle of poems within a dramatic framework. It is intended for performance in a theatre before an audience, but it also longs to be taken home and quietly revisited. The entire play is like a poem in that it creates an emotional moment through the ebb and flow, cadence and harmony of language much as the individual poems themselves hope to accomplish. See the images enacted on stage. Hear the words spoken. Feel the weight of the book in your hands. Read its pages with your own eyes, and if so moved, remember a line or a phrase in days to come.

The "poetry play" offers the full poetic experience. In this wonderfully rich time when every local café seems to hold its own series of poetry readings, when theatres and concert halls are filled with people listening to slam competitions, when poems can be found on commuter trains and in doctors' waiting rooms, the "poetry play" seems ripe for a renaissance. I hope *Dreams of May* can contribute to that revival.

Sue Guiney

Table of Contents

Inner Strength   11
Questions on a Train   13
The Honesty Bar   17
Pas de Fromage   19
The Gift   21
Seeing an Angel   23
His Heart   25
It's Not So Hard to Die   27
In the Dark   29
Withstanding   31
Curving Road   33
Collar Stays   35
I Didn't Really Want To   37
Upon Leaving   39
Villanelle   41
A Poem About Seeing   43
Reincarnation on a Blistering Day   45
The Traveler   47
The Mountain Climber   49
Latin Nights   51
Après Dessert   53
An Invocation   55

Characters

WOMAN, late 40's, not unattractive but plainly dressed so as not to call attention to herself (twin set, knee-length skirt, pearls, button earrings, nylons, pumps). She carries a large handbag in one hand; over her shoulder is a tote bag.

Set

A commuter train, with its usual random flickering lights, starts and stops, rocking and jostling, ambient noise. The set creates a simple, basic framework in which the character can free associate, remember, confront her past and begin to find her way forward. Like the jostling rhythm of the train, so do her thoughts jostle back and forth between distant memories, recent crises and insistent fantasies. She talks to herself.

The opening of a train car door is heard. The Woman walks down the aisle, finds a seat next to a window, and sits down. She looks around to see if anyone else might be coming to sit beside her. No one does. She puts her tote bag on the seat next to her and keeps her handbag on her lap. She sits very rigidly, with her feet on the floor and her back straight against the seat. She looks agitated. Perhaps she's been rushing. Eventually, with exasperation and resignation, she speaks.

Women can't swoon anymore.
Too bad.
People can't take to their beds,
Can't suffer nervous exhaustion,
Can't languish.

Now there is always a reason.
Symptoms follow pathology
like mice follow frosts.

I can't keep you out.

The Woman sits quite still, clearly ill at ease, and stares out the window. The train door slams and catches her attention. She noticeably stiffens as she follows with her eyes an unseen someone who walks through the car. She keeps staring until another car door slams hard. She looks frightened, but then shakes her head as if she was afraid she had recognized the person, but had then realized she hadn't. She takes a deep breath as if trying to relax, mutters to herself and then speaks her thoughts.

He looked like James Dean,
who looks like every aging, bewildered,
somehow dangerous young man
with tousled hair and watery, hurt eyes.

The train rocked with a rock'n roll rhythm.
He sat across from me, one row away.
His head bobbed to some imagined bass guitar riff.
I tried hard not to look.

"Do you know what time we get to Battersea?"
he asked some other middle-aged woman.
"Five minutes or so. We're almost there,"
I'm surprised to hear her answer.
"You know that Dog Shelter? It's famous, right?"
He asked another question.
"Yes, I got my dog there," she answered him.

Doesn't she know not to talk to strange men?
Why did she smile? Why encourage him?
She looked like an ordinary person, much like me,
hair cut nicely by a local salon,
a tidy case of papers, books at her side.
I looked out the window, at factories passing by.

The train soon stopped. They both got up to stand by the
    door.
An older woman filed in behind them. Her hair was
white/grey in short, tight curls. Her bag white plastic, from
    Woolworth's.
"Do you know what time it is? I've lost my watch."
Now he's talking to her, and not only does she answer,
she smiles.

They chatted about nothing as we all walked down the
    platform.
I heard a high-pitched laugh from her, a deep-throated
    chuckle
from him.

Hours later, I was still uneasy.
Why weren't those women afraid?
He had cigarette-stained fingers,
nothing but a ticket in his hand.
He could have asked them for money,
even followed one of them home.

Who was he, but a sinister-looking,
almost dirty,
older-than-he-seemed,
unknown-quantity-of-a-man,
alone on the edge of his seat in a train?

And why didn't he talk to me?

The Woman rummages through her purse, looking for her lipstick and compact. She finds them and puts the lipstick on, being sure to apply it neatly and carefully, and then places her things back in her bag. She looks around and notices a Travel and Leisure magazine left behind on the seat beside her. She picks it up and starts to thumb through it. While reading, she looks back in her bag for her handkerchief, which she pulls out and uses, dabbing at her nose and, perhaps, an eye. Replacing it in her bag, she unexpectedly comes upon a book of matches. She laughs in surprise, holds it in her hand, turns it over and over to read the print. It triggers a memory. She looks dreamily as she speaks.

There was an honesty bar
in a little hotel
at the back of the Place des Vosges.

Take what you want, sign your name.
The offerings were tantalizing:
two bottles of wine, three kinds of whisky,
liqueurs I didn't recognize.

But honestly, I wanted Pernod,
wanted to sit with a glass smelling of liquorice,
pour water in and watch the world become a cloud.

To be really honest . . .
I wanted absinthe, whatever that it is,
illegal, I think, liquid opium, maybe,
that drink destitute Parisian writers shared
with bohemian women, a drink
to be afraid of, to speak French to
within a cloud of smoke.

I wanted to walk into the Place at night,
a little worse for wear,
and hear footfalls of horses on cobbled streets,

to see shadows of lovers beneath distant lamplights,
be the shadow of a lover beneath a distant lamplight,

wear a turban
and a slit up the side of my dress,
fishnet stockings and heels like poison-tipped arrows,

to sip absinthe within a surreal haze
and be lost within a romantic age.

Honestly, that's what I wanted.

The Woman remembers herself and continues to look for, and then find, her reading glasses. She puts them on and starts to thumb through the magazine. At a certain page, she stops. She talks to herself about what she is reading, muttering something like, 'Oh yes, I remember that restaurant...' Then she continues to speak.

From across the room
I can smell the cheese
which I don't allow myself
to eat.

Two mounds like breasts
beckon at me
from a host of blocks –
square, rectangular,
creamy, white,
speckled with regional herbs.
All fragrant beyond belief.

I don't let myself touch.
But I dream nonetheless
like some old man dribbling
in a greasy raincoat,
hidden around a brick corner,
smoking a soggy fag,

alert and alive but
alas, oh alas,
bereft.

She reads for a few more moments and then realizes she needs something else. She picks up her tote bag and begins to rummage through that. She finds her notebook and pen, and writes down the name of the restaurant. The notebook's bookmark is a feather which she abstractedly twirls in her hand. Eventually, she begins to look at it more closely. It jogs her memory.

Twitching on the ground,
wings wrinkled with indignation,
it lay
waiting
for my opened door.

In time I did open it,
thinking only of
cereal boxes, cat food,
toilet paper, a pint of milk.

My cat appeared.
She rubbed against my leg
demanding attention.
Her tail was erect,
her whiskers ready.

"What's this?" I asked out loud.
"A gift," she smiled and purred.
"I brought it just for you," she seemed to say.

Bending down to stroke the cat
I looked a little closer.
A bird or once-a-bird,
bloody, twitching, wrinkled,
lay like an ocean across my path.

"No," I screamed and slammed the door.
"How could you bring me such a gift?"
From behind safe curtains I peered outside
to see my cat still sitting there.

"How rude," she meowed with opened mouth,
her nose turned up with disapproval.
She carried off her prey and left me,
shaking and
alone.

She sits for a moment in a quiet melancholy, and then continues…

Sitting in the front seat of her new mini-van,
bags of old recycling at my feet,
she told me she had seen an angel.

It was years ago, on the side of the road,
in the middle of nowhere-America.
She was lost, my friend, and frightened, driving

beyond the limits of any known town.
The light was dancing between listing leaves.
It blinded her, she said.

Suddenly, a woman
along the road, thumb outstretched,
cigarette dangling from blood red lips

appeared in her rear-view mirror.
It was her mother's face, but younger, smoother,
as if from years forgotten, lost, barely ever believed. . .

or so she thought.
My friend pulled over, almost stopping,
wanting to ask, "Can I help?"

But the woman was gone.
In her place, tricks of light
and beyond, just beyond

home.

She looks at the matches, which have remained in her lap, one more time and then puts them back in her bag. She is lost in thought and continues to herself.

His heart exploded one night,
exploding with it my childhood beliefs
that we all live until an aged end
and have quiet moments to say goodbye.

Now, a lifetime later,
I can still hear his giggle
bubbling from a smoky throat;
subversive jokes and a wink just for me
offered down like sweets
from a height I never reached.

I can hear his stubby nails, rough and unfiled,
their clackety staccato
tapping boogie woogie fugues
on the old upright piano in the corner.

I thought I said goodbye twenty years ago.
But I keep leaning forward
straining to hear
the echo of his answer in the air.

Angry now, she pauses for a moment and then speaks as if addressing the audience, although she is clearly chastising herself.

It's not so hard to die

think of the millions who've done it.
Ones who did well in school,
those who never finished, those who lived
their dreams, those who never dreamt
at all.

Being left behind is harder.

When you're the one left walking down
the cold hall to the toilet,
left to do the hoovering
or put petrol in the car,

sleeping on that bony mattress,
waiting for the plumber,

the smell of smoke, bomb threats,
fears in the middle of the night...

The Woman takes out her handkerchief once again. She dries her eyes, blows her nose. She is angry with herself, and now determined to regain her composure. She stands up, collecting her bags, her coat and the magazine. She looks around and moves to find another seat, perhaps as far as another car. As she walks, she speaks to herself, angrily muttering under her breath.

A star like tangled spider legs
refuses to shoot across the sky
but sits
half asleep   half broken
            splintered

Onoff onoff the flickering light
resists its obligation
to shine on me –

…I lose my way …

Where can I find clearness?
God-damned lazy star!

She continues to find a new seat, and eventually finds one to her liking, settling in as she speaks.

There's a boulder on the beach.
But "boulder" sounds massive, weighty, permanent.
Actually, it's rather small, but sturdy
and stubborn.

Throughout the day, throughout the night
as minutes tumble headlong into tomorrow
the ocean unloads itself --
the silt, the stones, the salt, the skeletons,
the history of the earth, the answers to our questions
all on its head.

All time -- forever, unending, eternal, incessant. . .

"Will I, too, endure?"

The Woman takes a deep breath, trying to calm herself. She sits up straight and does what it takes to make herself look as if she is fine, although she isn't. She slowly turns the pages of the magazine, humming a tune as she reads. She nods and smiles, pretending that the article she is reading has captured her attention, but her rigid, tense body shows that she is still distressed. In time, she begins to look for something in her handbag again. Some things she takes out she quickly puts aside -- "normal" things like a pack of tissues, lipstick, a hairbrush. She pulls out her notebook again. In between two of the pages is a pressed flower. As she continues to look closely at the flower, she absent-mindedly places her other things back into her bags.

The curving road by my front door
looks nothing like it did before,
when fits of spring brought newborn green
and blossoms peeked from in-between.

Then, my front door was opened wide
to welcome all my friends inside
to white-washed walls and sun-filled space,
an accepting heart for every face.

The table, then, was always filled
with vases full of wild dill,
stalks of basil, fresh-cut thyme,
mosaic bowls of Moroccan lime.

One meal flowed into the next,
an extra plate for one more guest,
when my front door was opened wide,
the flowered road curving beside.

But once the blossoms fall away
and winter kills the dreams of May,
my house lies still in empty cold
and frost heaves crack the curving road.

I gaze outside in hopes of cheer
but no one cares to travel near.
My yearning heart may dream in vain,
but the house, the road and I remain.

The Woman stares out the window, completely lost in thought. She puts the pressed flower in a special front pocket of her handbag as if not to lose it again. While she is doing that, she finds a dry cleaning ticket. She sighs deeply, shakes her head.

He once made a mess with his collar stays
on the bathroom counter.
Bits of oddly-shaped plastic
scattered like fallen leaves.

It was surprising to see them there,
to see anything of his so out of order,
so slapdash, helter skelter.

At first I thought I'd yell or be sarcastic.
"Look at the mess you made" or simply
"And who's to clean this up, then?"

But then I thought I'd let it lie
and hope he rushes off to work without the urge
to recreate order,

to control the uncontrollable
and impose his enormous will.
His life is tidy enough.

Where is that old, wild smile of his,
a man on the beach,
long hair spraying in every direction,
laughing,
having forgotten his pants?

The Woman continues to stare off into space, shaking her head. She soon continues speaking, as if confessing.

I didn't really want to
rifle through his pocket.

But the comforting cashmere
of the half-folded flap,
the creamy silk of the
slightly bulging lining

made my hand twitch with nervous hysteria,
my calm mind spin with lethal imaginings.

She now stares at the audience and speaks intently.

Imagine a cut,
straight and clear,
like two panes of glass nestled together,
touching.

Each with its longings and allegiances.

Now imagine a heart, split,
not broken.
A jagged cut runs through the core.
No steady hand could join it.

Never again whole.

She puts the ticket away, mumbling to herself something like, 'Forget it. It's hopeless.' She then speaks.

Do not be angry when I have to leave.
Your eyes will still pop open every day.
You'll see, I'll be the one who's left to grieve.

Don't cling so tightly to my tattered sleeve.
In time, I know, you won't want me to stay.
Do not be angry now that I must leave.

We've worked so hard to make our futures weave
a cloth to shield us both. But now it frays.
You'll see, I'll be the one who's left to grieve.

Our youthful road seemed easy to perceive.
But now time crumbles off like hardened clay.
Do not be angry that I have to leave.

I loved you with a force I can't conceive.
I beg you, take what's left and step away.
You see, I'll be the one who's left to grieve.

My eyes are full of tears. Ignore them, please.
With backward steps I release you from today.
Do not be angry when I have to leave.
You'll see, I'll be the one who's left to grieve.

She stares down at her feet. The movement of the train jolts her back and forth. Eventually, she picks up her magazine once again and reads. Actually, she now seems more relaxed. Her body is less stiff. Perhaps she even leans back and smiles as she turns the pages. She finds something that catches her interest and she tears it out. She stares at it as she speaks.

I read a poem about seeing.
Once in a word the image startled my eye,
another bored it, trancelike,
with its everyday.

But I like the idea.

What do we want to see?
Not what we do see:
>rows of schoolgirls outstretched hands gypsy
>women Ford Fiestas white beribboned hats
>cradling sun-starved streets squatting on
>purple infants dirty heads scattered spangled
>pence

What do I want to see?

I want to see a poem.

The Woman reads the magazine with greater interest and attention now, tearing out advertisements, marking up pages. Something she reads sparks her imagination. She mutters to herself about it, and then, speaks as if recalling a memory.

The air is water
outside the window.

The force of my sigh gives me
blowfish lips.

She sighs, puckers.

Through the haze comes summer sounds of
clanging flagpoles, clicking flip flops,
the caw-caw of a seagull.
It pulls my eyes to a nearby roof.

First there is nothing, then a slow approach of white.
Strolling, not flying, he casually appears,
wings swept back like hands thrust in pockets,
a sideways glance from an up-turned head.

"It's Fred Astaire in bird form," I cry.
I swear he winks at me. I laugh.
My heart flies up to greet him.

The Woman now becomes completely engrossed in her magazine. She settles into her seat, turning fully towards the window, with her back to her bags and the aisle of the train car. She turns a few more pages of the magazine and then looks up in reverie.

My, I love hotels.

(The expensive kind, I mean,
 lobbies full of chandeliers,
quilted leather hassocks,
carpets of inlaid Persian reds and blues.)

I love the promise of a marble bathroom.

(Perhaps, a secret try at a bidet.
Coloured bottles of narrow curves
with golden fluids of molten velvet
send a tingle to my balding scalp.)

I've been known to take photographs of closets.

(Rows of satin-covered hangers
are waiting, waiting just for me
and my crush-proof reversible jacket, hidden pockets.)

And if there's a terrace, even better.

Then I stand outside, if the weather's fine,
leaning over a filigreed railing,
and dream myself into another century . . .

some former life where others live to service
my whims,
and the world holds its breath to hear
my plans,
daughters bow their spirits before
my spirit.

And I always always always
come first.

The Woman flips through the magazine some more and finds another page which reminds her of something. She continually makes comments to herself about what she is reading.

My lips are burning
red and sore, they beg
the soothing balm of
greasy, stinging salve.

But, I don't mind.
This is what mountains do.

Now, like every year, I pull on
layers of insulated cotton,
wide-woven Gortex,
knee-length tightly knit socks.
One last scratch to the itching ankle welts and
I'm ready.

Not for battling the elements;
everyday life challenges me enough.

But instead to come and stand
on top of this snow-covered mountain,
look beyond into the depths of remote Italy,
and despite feeling minute within
the expanse of white-blue silence,
I believe I am also

brave
strong
capable
bold
briefly   momentarily
in charge.

She closes her eyes as if to better visualize her memory, but the swaying of the train actually puts her to sleep. The lighting changes to indicate that she is dreaming. Latin music starts softly and then increases in intensity. Still dreaming, she stands up and begins to dance to the music in her dream. She continues to dance as she speaks.

Latin nights.
That pulsing beat.
The smell of sweat.
Yes,
Hot, dripping, pulsing.

The bandleader, unbuttoned shirt,
Dark eyes.
He winds his way towards me.
He sizzles.

He reaches for me.
I reach for him.
Bending over me.
Swirling me away.

My leg comes up,
Tightly around him.
Dipping.
Pulsing.
Stabbing.
Deep.

I am his dream.

She continues to dance. Eventually, the music grows quieter and the light fades. The Woman dances herself back to her seat. When the music stops, she wakes up, surprised that she had actually been asleep, slightly embarrassed, but still smiling. Taking a breath to bring herself back to reality, she smoothes out her skirt, puts back on the cardigan she had flung off as she danced, fixes her hair. The music is gone. All that can be heard is the noise from the train. But The Woman still smiles. She finds her lipstick and puts it on, using the window as a mirror. She kicks off her shoes and tucks her legs up under her as she starts to read the magazine again. She stops at a page and looks at it longingly. It makes her look through her bag again and pulls out a candy bar. She looks at it before she eats.

"Après dessert."
What a concept!
As if the chef was telling me
"… there's no such thing as too much.
This meal can go on forever
and we will never feel pain or remorse
or the shaft of regret in our hearts."

Close your eyes.
Imagine eternity.
With you
and a *tarte de pomme*,
glace vanille creamier than heaven,

and me
alive, young
always content,
never full.

She begins to eat the candy, but in a few moments, the train stops. She is surprised. It's her stop. Quickly, she gathers up her shoes, her bags, her coat. She rushes off towards the train door. She starts to put the magazine in her bag, but then decides to leave it behind for the next person. As she gets closer to the door, the music from before gets slowly louder, coming from nowhere. She hears it and looks around, trying to see where it is coming from. Maybe from beyond the train door? She reaches for the handle. Just as she starts to turn it, she speaks.

Hear that sound, that music?
Bring it to me.

Golden like a spark shedding light,
just a little, but enough to show
the corner of the thought.

It is hope returning.
easier to hold than joy,
slick and slipping from my heart.

But there it is. Do you hear it?
Do you?

She opens the door. Immediately, the stage goes dark and the music stops.